T0199004

LAUREL KHIABANI

FINDING YOUR (LOST) JOY

To order additional copies of this book, contact:
Xlibris
1-888-795-4274
www.Xlibris.com
Orders@Xlibris.com

ISBN: 978-1-9845-8253-9 (sc)
ISBN: 978-1-9845-8254-6 (hc)
ISBN: 978-1-9845-8255-3 (e)

Print information available on the last page

Rev. date: 06/15/2020

Finding Your (Lost) Joy

By Laurel Khiabani

Finding Your (Lost) Joy: Lola's Big Book of Love

By Laurel Khiabani

Dedicated with eternal gratitude ever after to Amir for his enormous role in our fairytale dream marriage, to Chris for showing up to support and encourage me, and to Mike, whose kindness helped me through the toughest part of this heart-wrenching journey;

Thank you all for the insightful lessons that changed my life forever.

These are the things that bring joy to my heart. There is a lot of room in the boxes so that you can write in what brings joy to you. Then you can read it tomorrow or any day you feel down, to lift your spirits and make this book your own.

Love that overflows your heart	Peaceful serenity and quiet of undisturbed snow.

Baby Kara's and Kaycie's laughter	The air's newness after the rain

Knowing that you get me and you love me.	Knowing we're on each other's team.

Embraces from My Beloved	Knowing my worth

Knowing My Purpose	Noticing how big the moon is tonight

This marriage was like a fairy tale dream come true	Profound blessing when East meets West

Finished my best drawing ever

Found the perfect sand dollar

Found the perfect sea urchin shell and a starfish

Feeling safe with you and because of you

I love with my whole heart	We love each other with our whole hearts

Knowing you have my back	A sister who was there for me when I truly needed her

The way sand pipers scurry

I rushed in

I'm all in, and you're all in

Finger painting

Jane Austen	Parents that loved and encouraged me

Parents that made me feel loved and safe	My Father was dependable, thoughtful and generous

My Mother who encouraged me to develop my talents and loved to go exploring

Love that feels like my heart will burst

Look on Kara's face when she 1st learned to walk

Receiving a kind and supportive text from you

My happy place	Time shared together with my best friend

The elegant beauty of an orchid	The joyful and loving smile on your face

Breath-taking view from Coit Tower

The best cappuccino I ever had

Enjoying him, heart soul, and body

You know I'm here for you

Feeling of flow when I am super focused	Incredible longing for you when we are apart
Trying to mend the crack in the universe when you left	My love and family are divinely protected

Knowing my Love and family are well, happy, staying safe and prosperous

Remembering all my blessings and being happy in spite of …

We are helping each other heal through unconditional love

The thought of seeing him again soon

No fear	Knowing you will prevail
Knowing how much they care about you; you are not alone	Knowing you can do this

Knowing you will always have a home here

Hoping we can be better together

Letting go of senseless feelings of betrayal and abandonment brought on by his death

Knowing true love doesn't keep score

Making snow angels	Surprisingly powerful longing I have for you when we are apart

Knowing love is worth the risk	Knowing I have the courage to love again

Knowing I can trust you with my heart	Sometimes the way I feel about you scares me
Knowing how much I love Him	Knowing I need to stop worrying about you; God is taking care of you

Justice for you and living the dream	Thinking about you and praying you are safe
The man I fell for makes the world a better place and makes me want to be a better woman	The man I love is supportive, nurturing and kind

Our path is chosen from our hearts desire and what makes sense

You can handle my intensity

I become telepathic or you tell me how you feel about me and how you feel about us

My Love is loyal, honest and brilliant

I am all in; when we come together it will be mind, heart, body, and soul

He knows I think he's beautiful

He will be gentle if he thinks I may be scared; I will be gentle with him too

We share what we like and don't like to create harmony

Blissful, phenomenal 5D connection	Knowing the power of expansion (not going with the flow)

Recognizing power in service (no longer wallowing in the pain)	Knowing my best most joyful love-filled life is with my true love soulmate

You tell me how you truly feel about me
and I tell you how much I love you

Loving my true love soulmate unconditionally

All day with you

You know I love you just as you are

| | I feel you here; it's wonderful |
| Only you | |

| We value each other highly and have true intentions for exclusive long term relationship | Playing with you |

Connecting every day	We realize the different ways our plans will elevate our happiness

So grateful for friends and family that were there for me when I faced dark night of the soul	Manifesting you in all 7 chakras

Knowing I need to follow the path guided by love (for the greater good)

Listening to, hearing, and following my inner voice brings calm and peace

No drama and no fear

He loves me in a big protective way and so wants to be exclusive

There's something sacred and spiritual
about our feelings and love for each other

Our pure true love makes us want to protect
and guard each other's hearts and feelings

This love feels like heaven

Wanting you and having you
any day, all day, every day

Intentions to strive for and to get better every day	Hearing from you when you're away so I know that you're OK

Knowing that I am not alone	Knowing that we have so much to learn from each other and hoping there is enough time

What is happening in 5D	Anticipation of 1st kisses, caresses and hugs; hoping I won't just melt when you touch me

Knowing we can grow and heal together	Knowing we share joy, responsibilities and problems; we are team us.

You are ready and elated when my wave of genuine love comes crashing into you

My unconditional love for you makes you want to be better every day

I need you in my life because I love you

Look what you've done to me

'Seems like I'm taller

I love you so much that I want you to be fulfilled and happy whether we walk this path together or take separate roads

I see you

Love + Service + Surrender = Abundance

It's not so weird to hug a tree, as we are all one in the continuum

Knowing I am healing by loving myself unconditionally to be better and elevate

Waking up feeling a gentle wave of love, serenity, and light washing over me

The journey

Power of love is in the peace it brings	Surrendering
Phenomenal ethereal love I have for you	My unconditional love for you and others can heal my broken heart

The Tale of
Loveth
and
Diana

Ng Dagreat

Printed in the United States
By Bookmasters

Printed in the United States
by Baker & Taylor Publisher Services